ITALIAN
COOKING CLASS

Authentic Rustic Cucina

Contents

For further information contact Mirko Grillini at: **mianda@bigpond.com**
Tableware courtesy of MYER STORES
Cookware courtesy of ESSTEELE COOKWARE

Coordinator: Vicki Bright
Art Director: Karen Moores
Graphic Designer: Andrew Cunningham
Photography: Tony Gwynn Jones
Editor: Stefan Treyvaud

Italian Cooking Class
Published in 2004 by Hinkler Books Pty Ltd
17–23 Redwood Drive
Dingley VIC 3172 Australia
www.hinklerbooks.com

ISBN: 1 7412 1504 8
Printed and bound in China

Black Pearl Epicure & Cooking School

Babak Hadi is one of Australia's leading purveyors of fine foods. From his inner city premises, Black Pearl Epicure, Babak operates Brisbane's most exclusive gourmet retail outlet, and the internationally renowned Black Pearl Cooking School.

Cooking school manager **Vicki Bright** engages Australia's leading chefs for classes that combine education with social interaction. The School caters for individuals with a passion for food and a desire to learn about the wonderful ingredients available and how to use them.

Mirko Grillini's extremely popular pasta-making classes at Black Pearl Cooking School have been a huge success with constant demand for the sell-out classes. His hands-on approach and amicable teaching skills have made this one of the School's most popular and successful classes.

Black Pearl Epicure & Cooking School
36 Baxter Street, Fortitude Valley
Brisbane, Queensland
07 3257 2144
www.blackpearl.com.au
vicki.bright@blackpearl.com.au

Mirko Grillini

Born in Bologna in northern Italy, where he lived for 22 years, Mirko Grillini is an award-winning chef and cooking instructor with an enormous passion for rustic Italian food.

Mirko takes the simplest approach to cooking in the knowledge that the freshest and best quality ingredients combined with a long history of tradition will ensure a tasty and healthy dish. His drive and passion to teach others about the flavours of his home town and the surrounding region of Emilia-Romagna are second to none.

Mirko's Nonna (grandmother) taught him to make pasta by hand when he was a teenager. Mirko went on to work in the kitchens of San Lorenzo in London, before arriving in Australia and opening in Queensland the multiple award-winning Italian restaurant Nonna Pia.

Mirko now conducts cooking classes around the country, sharing his immense knowledge of authentic rustic Italian from pasta to tiramisu and everything in between.

Contact: mianda@bigpond.com

king school

Introduction to Italian

In Italy the *Accademia Italiana della* works to preserve the art of Italy's rustic and traditional cuisine.

Italy's 20 regions each produce authentic Italian cuisine specific to their location in respect of the ingredients and the seasons. The use of fresh ingredients ensures full flavour and healthy eating. **Simplicity is the key.**

Traditional rustic dishes were born of necessity. Butter was used less in the South because of the heat while the North used a great deal of dairy products. A polenta dish, now popular in contemporary restaurants, was once the poorest of meals, complemented only by a stew of game or poultry.

Rustic Italian food is not only regional, it is also specific to city and village. Common to all Italian cooking is the pleasure of cooking, taking pride in offering your guests or family a special meal.

Con la pancia piena le testa ragiona meglio.

WITH A FULL BELLY THE BRAIN MAKES MORE SENSE
NONNO (MIRKO GRILLINI'S GRANDFATHER)

ITALY
0 25 50 75 100 125 150 KM
MILES
0 25 50 75
N
Bologna
San Marino
ADRIATIC SEA
Roma
Bari
Naples
SARDINIA
ITALY
Population 57,956,000
SICILY
MEDITERRANEAN SEA
IONIAN SEA

ONE
Primi

TRADITIONALLY AN ITALIAN meal would begin with antipasto or pasta. The entrées suggested here offer lighter options to start a complete meal or can be served for a light lunch. A larger portion size can be used for a main meal.

Crostini agli Asparagi

ASPARAGUS CROSTONI (pictured opposite)

12 blanched asparagus spears (see basic recipes)
50g unsalted butter
100g pancetta slices roughly chopped
100g parmesan shaved
1 field mushroom, thinly sliced
1 garlic clove, crushed
100ml white wine
salt and pepper
1 loaf bread, ciabatta or similar, thinly sliced
olive oil

Cut 9 asparagus spears into small pieces, about 1/2cm in size.

Cut remaining 3 spears in half and put aside for garnish.

In a medium size frying pan, heat the butter, add pancetta and stir for 1 minute. Add mushrooms and asparagus. When the mixture is very hot add the wine then garlic and reduce to a thick creamy sauce.

Add the parmesan, (leave some for garnishing) salt and pepper.

To assemble, brush one side of the bread slices with olive oil then toast both sides until golden. Top oiled side of bread with asparagus mixture. Sprinkle with parmesan and garnish with remaining asparagus spears.

Terrina di Salmone

SALMON TERRINE

800g Atlantic salmon fillet (skin off, remove bones)
100ml fish stock
1 litre water
250g ricotta
50g capers
3 eggs
150ml whipping cream
1 large zucchini, finely sliced
1 large fennel bulb, finely sliced
ground white pepper
salt
1 tablespoon parsley, finely chopped
50g butter
100ml white wine

Preheat oven to 180°C.

In a pan large enough to fit the salmon fillet, bring water and stock to the boil then turn heat down to a simmer. Poach salmon fillet in pan for approximately 1 minute. Remove fillet and blend in food processor until smooth.

In a large frying pan add the butter and sauté fennel and zucchini. Season with salt and pepper then add wine and simmer for approximately 15 minutes or until the wine has evaporated.

In a stainless steel bowl mix the ricotta, capers, parsley and egg yolks. Whip the cream until slightly thickened then add to ricotta mix. Whip egg whites until firm then fold into ricotta with the processed salmon.

Line a terrine loaf with foil, allowing enough foil to overlap and cover the terrine completely. Grease foil with butter and dust with flour.

Place a quarter of the zucchini and fennel slices at the bottom of the tray then cover with a layer of salmon mix. Alternate between vegetable and salmon layers.

Fold the foil to cover the terrine and place in a bain-marie (a larger tray half filled with water).

Cook in oven for one hour. Let rest for an hour. Turn loaf upside down to release terrine and remove foil. Serve in slices.

Insalata di Gamberoni

PRAWN SALAD (pictured opposite)

2 large potatoes, boiled until skin is semi-soft
olive oil
100ml red wine
300g cleaned baby octopus
½ lemon
18 green king prawns shelled and de-veined
2 birds eye chillies, seeds removed, finely chopped
3 garlic cloves, crushed and finely chopped.
1 tablespoon parsley, finely chopped
100ml white wine
100ml olive oil
juice of 1 lemon
salt and pepper
300g rocket

Preheat oven to 200°C.

Peel the potatoes and slice into wedges. Rub with salt and olive oil, place in oven tray and bake until crisp (approximately 20 minutes).

Meanwhile ¾ fill a medium saucepan with water and add red wine.

Bring to the boil then add half a lemon and the octopus. After 15 minutes remove from heat. Drain octopus and leave to cool.

Heat olive oil in a frying pan. Add prawns and chili and when the prawns change colour, add octopus. Add white wine and garlic and reduce to a thick sauce. Add parsley and season with salt and pepper.

Mix rocket leaves, prawns, octopus, lemon juice and pan juices in a bowl. Serve with potatoes.

Vellutata al Finocchio

SILKY FENNEL SOUP

2 large fennel bulbs, halved, finely sliced
2 brown onions, finely sliced
100g unsalted butter
3 carrots, peeled and thinly sliced
1 litre chicken stock (see basic recipes)
1 litre milk
1 tablespoon white pepper
200g grated parmesan
salt to taste
1 tablespoon finely chopped parsley

Melt butter in a large pot. Add onions, fennel and carrots, stirring occasionally until soft.

Add stock and milk and bring to boil. Turn heat down and let simmer until the vegetables are cooked. Add parmesan, salt and pepper.

Blend in a food processor until smooth.

Serve in bowl. Garnish with parsley.

Peperoni Ripieni

STUFFED CAPSICUM (pictured opposite)

150g white bread, crusts removed
50ml milk
300g pork mince
300g veal mince
2 tablespoons chopped rosemary
1 tablespoon chopped oregano
salt and pepper
3 red capsicum

Soak bread in milk until it is soft (approximately 30 minutes).

In a bowl combine pork, veal, rosemary, oregano, salt, pepper and bread. Mix well and place in the fridge for 1 hour.

Preheat the oven to 200°C.

Cut the capsicum in half lengthways. Remove seeds and membrane. Fill the capsicum with the mince.
Place on an oven tray lined with foil.

Bake for approximately 30 minutes or until the mince is cooked.

Carpaccio di Tonno é Asparagi

TUNA CARPACCIO WITH ASPARAGUS

600g tuna fillet
100g baby capers
12 blanched asparagus spears (see basic recipes)
100g unsalted butter
1 lemon
100ml white wine
salt and pepper

Wrap the tuna tightly in cling film and place in freezer for half an hour.

Melt butter in a frying pan capable of fitting the asparagus without bending. Add asparagus and coat completely with butter. Deglaze pan with wine then add juice of 1/2 a lemon. Season with salt and pepper then remove from heat and let cool.

Remove tuna from freezer and slice thinly (about 3mm).

Cut the asparagus in half lengthways. Place asparagus and tuna in alternate layers on a serving plate. Top with capers and juice of remaining lemon half.

Serve cold.

Insalata di Cipolla e Tonno

TUNA SALAD (pictured opposite)

1 litre chicken or vegetable stock (see basic recipes)
500g tinned tuna (preserved in extra virgin olive oil)
2 Spanish onions, finely sliced
100g baby rocket leaves
200g borlotti beans, fresh or dried
100ml extra virgin olive oil
50ml balsamic vinegar
salt and white pepper

If using dried borlotti beans, soak them in water overnight.

Place beans, stock and a quarter of the onion in a deep pot with water and boil for 1 hour.

Drain the stock and let beans cool.

When cooled, combine beans with tuna (strain oil) and remaining ingredients in a large stainless steel bowl.

Season with salt and pepper.

Minestrone Rustico

RUSTIC MINESTRONE SOUP

200g spinach leaves, chopped in very small strips
600g angel hair pasta
300g dried beans, soaked in water for at least 12 hours
300g potatoes, cut into small cubes
80g pancetta, cut into small cubes
1 onion, finely chopped
1 tablespoon tomato paste, diluted in 100ml cold water
100g lard or butter
Grana Padano, grated
salt

In a large deep pan melt the lard and soften the onion. Add the pancetta and cook for about 2 minutes. Add the spinach and cook for a further minute. Add the diluted tomato paste, stir well and then add potatoes and beans.

Stir and cook for 5 minutes then add 2 litres of water and a good pinch of salt. Bring to the boil, then simmer for 2 hours. Add the angel hair pasta and cook until pasta is done. (see packet for timing)

Serve hot garnished with Grana Padano.

TWO

Sides

Peperoni in Festa
CAPSICUM PARTY

Zucchini al Burro
BUTTERED ZUCCHINI

Polento con Formaggio e Spinach
SPINACH & CHEESE POLENTA

22/23

Fascine di Carote e Fagiolini
CARROT & BEAN BUNDLES

Asparagi al Vino Bianco
ASPARAGUS IN WHITE WINE

Cipolle alle Erbe
HERBED SPANISH ONIONS

24/25

Funghi é Sedano
SAUTÉED MUSHROOMS

Melanzane alla Griglia
CHAR-GRILLED EGGPLANTS

Pure allo Zafferano con Piselli
MASHED POTATOES WITH SAFFRON & PEAS

26/27

A RUSTIC ITALIAN MEAL includes a selection of side dishes placed in the middle of the table for self-service, much like a buffet. Mix and match the side dishes to suit the meal ensuring that you offer complementary flavours as well as balanced weight to the meal.

Peperoni in Festa

CAPSICUM PARTY

25g unsalted butter
25g olive oil
200g prosciutto, sliced into 2cm strips
100g pine nuts
40 cooked and peeled broad beans (see basic recipes)
3 peeled yellow capsicum (see basic recipes)
3 peeled red capsicum
100ml wine
salt and white pepper

Cut prepared capsicum into strips approximately 1 cm wide.

In a large frying pan heat butter and oil.

Add prosciutto and pine nuts. Sauté until lightly coloured.

Add broad beans and capsicum. Sauté for 2 minutes.

Deglaze pan with wine.

Season with salt and pepper. Serve hot.

Zucchini al Burro

BUTTERED ZUCCHINI

12 medium zucchini
1 tablespoon olive oil
1 small red chilli, deseeded and sliced
2 garlic cloves, crushed
1 tablespoon parsley, finely chopped
100ml white wine
salt and white pepper

Cut the zucchini in half and then slice again length ways into 4 pieces.

Heat oil in a large frying pan. Sauté zucchini, garlic and chilli for 3 minutes.

Deglaze pan with wine and add parsley.

Season with salt and pepper.

Polento con Formaggio e Spinach

SPINACH & CHEESE POLENTA (pictured opposite)

600g polenta, cooked as per packet instructions
2 bunches fresh English spinach, blanched or two packets frozen spinach, thawed
150g Grana Padano, grated
50g unsalted butter
1 chilli, very finely sliced, seeds removed
salt

Melt unsalted butter in a large frying pan and panfry chilli for 1 minute then add spinach and sauté until steaming. Remove from heat, add half the grated Grana Padano and stir until the cheese is melted.

Season cooked polenta and spinach with salt.

Serve polenta topped with spinach and garnished with remaining Grana Padano.

Fascine di Carote e Fagiolini

CARROT & BEAN BUNDLES (pictured opposite)

54 green beans, topped and tailed
3-4 large carrots, peeled and cut into 36 logs the same length as the beans
200g flat pancetta, very thinly sliced
1 litre chicken stock
2 garlic cloves, crushed and finely chopped
100ml white wine
50ml extra virgin olive oil
black cracked pepper
salt

Bring the stock to boil in a large pot. Add carrots and beans and boil for 5 minutes.

Remove carrots and beans from stock. Note this stock can be kept for use in another recipe.

In a large pan heat oil and add carrots and beans. Sauté for 2 minutes to coat well with oil.

Splash with wine to deglaze pan. Before wine has completely evaporated add garlic and sauté for 2 minutes.

Season with salt and pepper.

Wrap 18 bundles of 2 carrot logs and 3 beans with pancetta.

As an alternative, sprinkle the bundles with parmesan and bake for 5 minutes.

Serve 3 bundles per person.

Asparagi al Vino Bianco

ASPARAGUS IN WHITE WINE

30 asparagus spears (5 per serve)
3 hot chillies, very finely sliced
100g unsalted butter
100ml white wine
50g Grana Padano, grated.
cracked black pepper
salt (preferably flakes)

Place asparagus in a large pot filled with water to about 1cm above the asparagus. Boil for 5 minutes then remove asparagus and discard water.

In the same pan melt butter at a low heat then add chilli and stir for 1 minute.

Add asparagus. Turn heat to medium and sauté gently ensuring the asparagus spears are well coated.

Deglaze pan with wine.

Take off heat and stir Grana Padano into asparagus, season with salt and pepper.

Cipolle alle Erbe

HERBED SPANISH ONIONS

3 large Spanish onions, finely sliced
20 leaves fresh marjoram or 2 teaspoons dry marjoram.
1 tablespoon fresh parsley, finely chopped
20 basil leaves, sliced
50ml extra virgin olive oil
100ml white wine
salt and white pepper

Heat oil in a large frying pan then add onion and sauté, stirring frequently to prevent browning.

Once the onion is softened add marjoram and parsley. Sauté for a further minute then deglaze pan with wine.

Add basil. Turn heat off and sauté for 10 seconds then season with salt and pepper.

Funghi é Sedano

SAUTÉED MUSHROOMS

50ml olive oil
20 button mushrooms, finely sliced
1 celery stalk, finely sliced
100ml chicken stock (see basic recipes)
2 garlic cloves , crushed and finely chopped
20 leaves fresh marjoram
2 tablespoons continental parsley, finely chopped
salt and pepper

Heat oil in pan and add mushrooms and celery.

Cook for approximately 5 minutes, stirring occasionally until the mushrooms are soft.

Add chicken stock, garlic and marjoram leaves. Simmer until the stock reduces.

Add parsley, season with salt and pepper.

Serve hot.

Melanzane alla Griglia

CHAR-GRILLED EGGPLANTS (pictured opposite)

2 medium size eggplants, sliced (see basic recipes)
2 garlic cloves, crushed
1 tablespoon continental parsley, finely chopped
200ml olive oil
salt and pepper

Cook eggplant on a char grill, barbecue or oven griller. Toss over heat with garlic, parsley and oil.

Season with salt and pepper.

Pure allo Zafferano con Piselli

MASHED POTATOES WITH SAFFRON & PEAS

6 potatoes
200g shelled and cooked peas
100g unsalted butter
1g saffron powder
200ml milk
100g grated parmesan
salt and pepper

Boil potatoes in their skins and peel while hot.

Mash potatoes with butter and gradually add milk.

Fold in peas, saffron and parmesan.

Season with salt and pepper.

THREE
Pasta

THE HEART OF ITALIAN cuisine, pasta dishes are the staple diet of most Italians. Traditionally served at the beginning of a meal, pasta dishes can also be served as a stand-alone meal. Remember the pasta is the main component of the dish. The sauce is not meant to 'drown' the pasta.

Tagliolini ai Porcini

TAGLIOLINI WITH PORCINI MUSHROOMS

50g grated parmesan
600g tagliolini
30g dried porcini mushrooms (soaked for 15 minutes in 500ml hot water)
6 diced roma tomatoes
3 garlic cloves, crushed and finely chopped
2 tablespoons chopped parsley
salt and pepper
50g unsalted butter
50ml olive oil

Bring a large pot of water to the boil. Add a good pinch of salt then add pasta. Follow cooking instructions on pasta packet and cook until al dente.

Heat the oil and butter in a pan.
Add drained porcini and sauté for 2 minutes.
Add the tomatoes and cook until soft. Add garlic and parsley.
Season with and salt and pepper.

Drain tagliolini, add to sauce, heat through and serve immediately.

Garnish with parmesan.

Taglietelle al Mascarpone

TAGLIETELLE WITH MASCARPONE (pictured opposite)

50g unsalted butter
600g fresh taglietelle (egg dough)
2 large field mushrooms, finely sliced
3 garlic cloves, finely sliced
2 large red capsicum (see basic recipes) sliced into 1/2cm strips
2 tablespoons chopped parsley
1 onion
750g mascarpone (Italian style)
100ml chicken stock
salt and pepper

Bring a large pot of water to the boil. Add a good pinch of salt then add pasta. Follow cooking instructions on pasta packet and cook until al dente.

In a large frying pan melt butter then add capsicum, onion, mushrooms, garlic and parsley. Sauté until vegetables are soft (do not brown) then add stock and simmer gently until evaporated.

Add mascarpone and let simmer until very hot. Season with salt and pepper.

Drain taglietelle, add to sauce, heat through and serve immediately.

Spaghetti alle Melanzane

SPAGHETTI WITH EGGPLANT (pictured opposite)

600g No 5 spaghetti
6 tomatoes, diced into small cubes
2 eggplants sliced 1cm thick (see basic recipes)
2 garlic cloves, finely chopped
3 chillies, finely chopped
30 sweet basil leaves, roughly chopped
50ml extra virgin olive oil
Parmigiano Reggiano to garnish
salt and white pepper

Bring a large pot of water to the boil. Add a good pinch of salt then add pasta. Follow cooking instructions on pasta packet and cook until al dente.

Char grill eggplant on barbeque or grill pan. Cut into small cubes.

Heat oil in a large frying pan then add chillies and leave for about 1 minute on low heat. Add tomato, eggplant, garlic and basil. Simmer for 3 minutes.

Drain spaghetti, add to sauce, heat through and serve immediately. Garnish with Parmigiano.

Penne alla Salsiccia

PENNE WITH ITALIAN SAUSAGES

50ml olive oil
600g penne rigate
500g plain Italian sausages, peeled and chopped into small chunks
3 zucchini, thinly sliced
3 garlic cloves, thinly sliced
30 basil leaves, roughly chopped
400ml cream
50g Grana Padano, grated
salt and pepper

Bring a large pot of water to the boil. Add a good pinch of salt then add pasta. Follow cooking instructions on pasta packet and cook until al dente.

Heat olive oil in a large frying pan and add sausages. Cook until medium rare.

Add zucchini and stir then add cream and garlic. Gently simmer for about 5 minutes to reduce. Add basil. Remove from heat and season with salt and pepper.

Drain penne, add to sauce with Grana Padano. Heat through and serve immediately.

Gnocchi alla Campagnola

FARMER'S STYLE GNOCCHI (pictured opposite)

500g gnocchi
50g unsalted butter
500g cooked broad beans
(see basic recipes)
100ml white wine
1 small onion, cut into slices,
½cm thick
3 garlic cloves, finely chopped
1g saffron threads
50ml cream
50g parmesan
salt and pepper

Melt butter in a pan and add onion. Cook until soft.

Add broad beans and saffron then splash with white wine. Add garlic while stirring then add cream and cook gently over low heat.

Bring a large pot of water to the boil. Add a good pinch of salt then add gnocchi. As the gnocchi rise to the surface, drain and add to the sauce.

Once all gnocchi is added stir to coat with sauce. Season with salt and pepper.

Garnish with parmesan.

Maccheroni al Forno

BAKED MACARONI

500g maccheroni
50g butter
1 litre besciamella/béchamel
(see basic recipes)
2 large field mushrooms, finely sliced
2 large onions, finely sliced
3 cloves garlic
2 tablespoons chopped parsley
150g sweet peas
200g honey ham, sliced about 3mm thick
and cut into squares
200g Grana Padano, grated
50ml unwooded white wine

Make béchamel sauce (see basic recipes).

Bring a large pot of water to the boil. Add a good pinch of salt then add pasta. Follow cooking instructions on pasta packet and cook until al dente.

Preheat oven to 200°C.

In a large frying pan melt butter and add onion and mushroom. Cook until soft, stirring occasionally. Add wine, garlic, peas and ham and simmer until wine has evaporated.

Add béchamel sauce and season with salt and pepper. Stir in parsley.

Grease the sides and bottom of an 8cm deep baking tray.

When the macaroni is cooked, drain and add to the sauce mixture. Mix well then add 100g of Grana Padano and mix again.

Pour into greased tray and sprinkle with remaining Grana Padano.

Bake in oven for 15 minutes.

FOUR
Secondi

ITALIAN DISHES ARE specific to each region, with seafood dishes served in coastal areas and dishes such as game meats served in the mountain regions. When deciding on a main meal consider your region's climate and the availability of fresh regional produce.

Pollo alla Zafferano

SAFFRON CHICKEN

1kg skinless chicken breasts
1g saffron threads
100g plain flour
100ml white wine
100ml chicken stock (see basic recipes)
1 onion, finely sliced
olive oil
salt and white pepper

Cut chicken breasts into 1cm strips, dip into flour, and shake off excess flour.

Heat oil in pan and soften onion then shallow fry chicken strips until golden brown. Splash with wine and let evaporate.

Dissolve saffron in the stock and add to chicken.

Simmer until the stock has reduced.

Season with salt and pepper.

Fagottini di Pollo

HERBED CHICKEN PARCELS

18 chicken drumsticks with skin
2 tablespoons parsley, very finely chopped
4 garlic cloves, crushed
1 tablespoon rosemary, finely chopped
50ml olive oil
salt and pepper
toothpicks

Using a sharp knife make an incision through the skin of the drumstick and remove skin carefully without tearing (see DVD). Cut the chicken meat from the bone and place in a food processor with parsley, garlic and rosemary. Season with salt and pepper. Mince mixture in food processor. Spoon into skins and secure with toothpicks.

Pan fry in oil until golden brown.

Filetto di Pesce al Pomodoro

FISH FILLETS IN TOMATO SAUCE (pictured opposite)

6 fish fillets (about 200g each)
500ml tomato purée
100g sugar peas
2 garlic cloves, chopped in half
1 tablespoon parsley, very finely chopped
100ml olive oil
2 birds eye chillies, finely chopped
salt
white pepper
50 g plain flour

Heat a large fry pan and add olive oil.

Add the garlic and fry until golden. Discard the garlic and add chili.

Dust fish with flour, shake off excess, and seal in pan for about 2 minutes each side. Remove fillets from pan and set aside.

Lower the heat and add the tomato purée to the pan. Add peas and parsley and simmer for a further 5 minutes to cook peas. Season with salt and pepper.

Return the fillets and cook until they almost fall apart. Turn to cook other side.

Risotto alla Parmigiana

BASIC RISOTTO

500g short grain rice (preferably Vialone Nano from a deli)
50g unsalted butter
100g Grana Padano
1 onion, finely chopped
200ml unwooded white wine
2 litres chicken stock, hot (see basic recipes)
salt

In a large pot melt butter and soften onion. Add rice and stir well until all grains are well coated with butter. Add wine and let evaporate. Add enough stock to cover rice by 1cm. Do not stop stirring.

Continue to add stock once it has been absorbed. The mixture should be a wet consistency at all times – not watery.

It will take about 20 minutes to cook.

After 15 minutes start tasting the rice. You want to reach a texture soft to bite yet still firm. Once you have added all the stock and the rice is cooked al dente remove from heat and add Grana Padano. Season with salt and serve immediately. Do not reheat.

Maiale al Miele

ITALIAN PORK CHOPS (pictured opposite)

6 pork chops (at least 200g each)
100g unsalted butter
150ml honey
70ml balsamic vinegar
2 tablespoons rosemary leaves
salt and pepper

In a large frying pan melt the butter. When hot, pan fry the chops for 3 minutes each side. Remove the chops, season with salt and put aside in a warm place.

Pour honey and balsamic into frying pan and bring to boil. Add rosemary and simmer for 5 minutes.

Add the rested chops and cook for 10 minutes continually coating with sauce.

Serve topped with juices left in pan.

Agnello Impanato

CRUMBED LAMB CUTLETS

12-18 lamb cutlets, fat removed
100g plain flour
4 eggs, beaten
30 fresh sage leaves finely chopped or
3 teaspoons dried sage
100g breadcrumbs
1 teaspoon nutmeg
200g butter
200g pancetta, cut into thin strips
400ml whole milk
salt and pepper

Place shallow baking tray in oven and preheat to 200°C.

Dust lamb cutlets with flour and shake off excess.

Combine breadcrumbs, half the chopped sage leaves, nutmeg and 1/2 teaspoon white pepper.

Dip cutlets into beaten egg mixture, then into crumb mixture. Shake to remove excess crumbs.

Heat a frying pan, add butter, then pancetta and remaining sage. Place cutlets in pan and cook until golden on both sides.

Place contents of pan into the hot oven tray.

Add milk covering the cutlets by three quarters. Place in oven and cook for 15 minutes.

Costata Ripiena

SAGE STUFFED VEAL CUTLETS (pictured opposite)

6 veal cutlets
12 fresh sage leaves or 1 teaspoon dried sage
100g talegio cheese
3 field mushrooms, sliced
splash white wine
2 garlic cloves, halved
50ml cream
salt and pepper
50g butter
olive oil

Preheat oven to 200°C.

With a sharp knife make an incision close to the bone of each veal cutlet. Stuff with sage (leave some sage for later) and cheese.

Heat oil in pan over moderate heat. When hot, seal and brown cutlets on either side.

Remove cutlets and rest for 5 minutes. Place cutlets on a heated oven tray and roast for 10-15 minutes.

Heat butter and oil in a fry pan over moderate heat. Add mushrooms, garlic and remaining sage. Sauté for 3 minutes. Deglaze pan with wine. Add cream, bring to boil then remove from heat. Season with salt and pepper.

In a food processor blend mushroom mix to a smooth consistency.

Remove cutlets from oven and rest for several minutes.

Serve each cutlet with the mushroom sauce.

Involtini agli Asparagi

VEAL WITH ASPARAGUS

12 veal slices (scallopine)
12 asparagus spears (see basic recipes)
12 slices mozzarella (3mm thick)
150ml white wine
50g plain flour
butter
salt and pepper
toothpicks

Sauté asparagus in butter, seasoned with salt and pepper, for 3 minutes. Set aside to cool.

Preheat oven to 200°C.

To assemble involtini place mozzarella on top of veal slices and asparagus spear on top of mozzarella. Roll the veal into a cigar shape and secure with a toothpick. Dust involtini (cigars) with flour then remove toothpicks, compressing the veal parcel with your hands.

Heat pan and melt butter. Pan fry the involtini both sides and deglaze pan with wine. Once brown remove veal from pan and place in a baking tray. Bake in oven for 5 minutes.

Polpettine al Latte

INDIVIDUAL VEAL MEATBALLS POACHED IN MILK (pictured opposite)

1.2kg veal mince
150g white bread, soaked in 100ml milk
5 garlic cloves, finely chopped
2 tablespoons fresh oregano, finely chopped
1 tablespoon fresh rosemary, finely chopped
1 litre milk
50ml olive oil
salt and pepper
flour

Preheat oven to 200°C.

Combine the veal mince, garlic, oregano and rosemary. Add soaked bread and combine well. Season with salt and pepper then rest the mixture for 30 minutes.

Form meatballs in your hands, about 100g each, and dust in flour, shaking off any excess.
Heat oil in frying pan and seal the meatballs until they reach a golden colour.

Place meatballs in oven tray, at least 8cm deep, and cover to halfway with milk. Bake in oven for about 25 minutes.

Medaglioni al Marsala

MARSALA BEEF MEDALLIONS

6 x 200g beef medallions
200ml marsala
2 rosemary sprigs
100ml chicken stock
50g butter
1 tablespoon corn flour

Preheat oven to 200°C.

Heat a pan and add butter. Seal medallions on either side. Leave to rest in a warm place.

Place chicken stock in a saucepan and bring to the boil. Add rosemary and marsala to the stock. Add corn flour and whisk to prevent lumps. Reduce heat and simmer for approximately 10 minutes until sauce thickens.

Finish medallions in oven for 10 minutes and serve with sauce.

FIVE

Dolci

WHILE ITALIANS HAVE a definite sweet tooth, cakes and desserts are most often served as a family treat on weekends and special occasions. Desserts are a wonderful way to complete a meal and let your palette know that the dining experience is over.

Torta al Cioccolato Bianco

WHITE CHOCOLATE TORTE (pictured opposite)

400g white chocolate
200g unsalted butter
150g plain flour
100g sugar
12 eggs
shaved white chocolate, for garnish

Preheat oven to 160°C.

Grease the base and sides of a 30cm cake tin with butter and dust with flour. Discard excess flour.

Place butter and chocolate in a stainless steel bowl over a pot of boiling water. The water should not touch the bowl.

When the butter and chocolate have melted stir with a wooden spoon and remove from heat.

Separate the eggs and add the sugar to the yolks. Whisk vigorously.

Add flour and keep whisking until mixture reaches a smooth consistency.

With a whisk or electric beater whisk whites until stiff peaks form. Fold the whites into the egg yolk mixture.

Pour into cake tin and cover with foil.

Cook for approximately 30 minutes or until the cake is springy when touched.

When cool, run a thin knife between cake and pan, unmould onto a rack and turn right side up.

Serve with shaved white chocolate.

Tiramisu

TIRAMISU

500g mascarpone
8 egg yolks
6 egg whites
80g icing sugar
600ml espresso coffee
90ml coffee liqueur
40 Savoiardi biscuits (available from good supermarkets and delis)
cocoa
20Wx25Lx10D cm baking tray

Place the egg yolks and whites into two separate stainless steel bowls. Add icing sugar to the yolks and whisk vigorously until creamy. Add mascarpone and whisk until creamy.

With a clean and dry whisk, beat the egg whites until they form a solid froth.

Gently fold the beaten egg whites into the mascarpone mix.

Soak the biscuits in the coffee until they absorb the liquid. Do not over soak or they will fall apart. Place the biscuits at the bottom of the tray and spread gently with a 1.5cm thick layer of egg mixture. Repeat for another two layers. Dust the final layer with cocoa and place in the fridge to set for approximately 6 hours.

Tortina di Mele

APPLE TART

300g caster sugar
150g soft butter
4 eggs
100 g plain flour
1 tablespoon corn flour
1/2 tablespoon baking powder
2 Granny Smith apples
300ml full cream milk

Preheat oven to 180°C.

Grease a rectangular baking tray.

Skin the apple and cut into quarters. Remove seeds and core. Dice into small pieces.

Cream butter and sugar, add eggs and milk and continue to mix. Sieve the flour, baking powder and corn flour into the wet mixture. Fold in apple and pour into rectangular tray.

Bake for 30 minutes or until firm.

Gelatina al Lamponi e Menta

RASPBERRY & MINT JELLY (pictured opposite)

300g raspberries, fresh or frozen
500ml water
3 tablespoons caster sugar
20 mint leaves, finely chopped
3 1/2 teaspoons gelatine powder

In a saucepan bring the water to the boil.

Add the raspberries and the sugar. Let simmer for about 5 minutes.

Add half the mint and simmer for 10 minutes.

Remove from heat, add gelatine and stir with a whisk to avoid lumps.

Add remaining mint.

Fill six individual moulds with the mixture and set in the fridge for 6 hours.

Sfrappole

SFRAPPOLE (pictured opposite)

3 eggs
350g plain flour
50g unsalted butter
1 teaspoon salt
30ml cognac or brandy
100g icing sugar
canola oil, for frying

Place flour in a bowl. Make a well, add eggs, melted butter, cognac and salt and mix to a dough with a fork. It should reach a non-wet consistency.

Roll the dough very thinly with a rolling pin.

Cut strips of about 4cm wide and 40cm long.

Make a wide knot with each strip and drop into hot oil in a fry pan.

The oil is at the correct temperature when the knot rises to the surface immediately. Don't let the oil smoke.

Remove bows from oil, drain on paper towel. Place on a cake rack and sprinkle with icing sugar.

Serve with coffee.

Sfrappole can be kept in an airtight container for several days.

Focaccia Dolci alle Albicocche

APRICOT FOCACCIA

500g plain flour
1/2 tablespoon salt
150g warm water
2 tablespoons olive oil
100g warm milk
10g dry yeast
4 tablespoons caster sugar
500g preserved apricots or peaches
2 stalks of rosemary

Preheat oven to 220°C.

Place flour, yeast and salt in a bowl and mix together. Gradually add water, olive oil and milk and mix with a fork until dough forms. Dough must be soft and elastic. Because flour varies, be prepared to add water or flour to reach the right texture.

In your hands roll the dough into a ball.

Lightly grease an oven tray large enough to spread the dough evenly with a thickness of about 2.5cm.

Strain the peaches or apricots and dry them completely.

Lay them in rows on the focaccia, cut side down.

Take the leaves of rosemary off the stalks and sprinkle them on the focaccia.

Sprinkle the sugar evenly over the top. Leave the dough to double in height.

When dough has risen, place in the oven for 15 minutes or until golden in colour.

Serve drizzled with honey.

Basic Recipes

Asparagus

Remove the woody base of asparagus spears by bending the spear between your thumb and forefinger until the asparagus snaps. You will find a natural weak spot at the base of the spear. To blanch, drop asparagus into a pot of boiling water. Return to the boil and cook for 2-3 minutes then remove asparagus and place in ice -cold water to stop the cooking process. Blanching cooks the asparagus while leaving it slightly crunchy.

Besciamella

Melt 100g unsalted butter in a pot then add 100g plain flour. This is called a roux. Cook the roux gently for 1 minute ensuring it doesn't burn then gradually add 1 litre of milk. As the sauce is heated the flour will begin to thicken the milk. For a lighter sauce you can use stock instead of milk.

Capsicum

Place the whole capsicum upside down on an oven tray and bake in a hot oven (200°C) until it becomes dark red to black – approximately 25 minutes. Remove capsicum from the oven. Once cooled the skin will peel away easily. Cut capsicum in half and remove seeds then use according to recipe.

Deglaze

Deglazing simply lifts all the tasty remnants of food from the base of a pan and incorporates them back into the dish. Add wine to the hot pan and move the liquid around the pan to collect the sediment. Let the wine evaporate completely, leaving a thickened sauce in the now 'clean' pan.

Eggplant

Cut eggplant into slices 1-2cm thick. Place them on a wire rack and sprinkle generously with salt. Leave for an hour. The eggplant will sweat, removing the bitterness. After an hour wipe salt and liquid off eggplant then cook as per recipe.

Stock

In a large heavy bottomed pot place two carrots, two sticks of celery and an onion – all cut into chunks. Fill with water and add main ingredient. For fish stock use a fish head or frame. For chicken use a whole raw chicken, preferably old. Bring to boil then simmer for 4-5 hours reducing the liquid to one-third its original volume. Strain stock from ingredients and use according to recipe.

Pasta

A good rule of thumb is to cook 200g of pasta in 2 litres of water. Bring the water to the boil then add a good pinch of salt. Add pasta and cook until al dente. Al dente literally means 'to the tooth'. The pasta should be tender but still firm to the bite. Most dried pastas require approximately 10 minutes of cooking. Fresh pasta cooks much faster than dried pasta. Refer to the cooking time on the pasta packet.

Menu & Wine Suggestions

Summer Seafood

CARPACCIO DI TONNO E ASPARAGI – Tuna Carpaccio with Asparagus
very crisp white, lean and not too fruity, eg young riesling , soave or pinot grigio

SPAGHETTI ALLE MELANZANE – Spaghetti with Eggplant
rosé

FILETTO DI PESCE AL POMODORO – Fish Fillets in Tomato Sauce
light red, eg beaujolais or light pinot noir

GELATINA AL LAMPONI E MENTA – Raspberry & Mint Jelly
Moscato di Asti

Winter Warmer

VELLUTATA AL FINOCCHIO – Silky Fennel Soup
crisp white, eg soave, pinot grigio, sancerre, New Zealand sauvignon blanc

TAGLIETELLE AL MASCARPONE – Taglietelle with Mascarpone
wooded white, eg chardonnay, barossa semillon

AGNELLO IMPANATO – Crumbed Lamb Cutlets with
Mashed Potatoes, Saffron,Peas and Buttered Zucchini
chianti or cabernet blends

TORTA AL CIOCCOLATO BIANCO – White Chocolate Torte
Spanish pedro ximinez, Australian sweet, sweet fortified

Two Course Lunch with Coffee

GNOCCHI ALLA CAMPAGNOLA – Farmer's Style Gnocchi

rustic white, eg cotes du rhone blanc

COSTATA RIPIENA and MELANZANE ALLA GRIGLIA – Sage Stuffed Veal Cutlets with Char-grilled Eggplants

medium bodied red, sangiovese di romagna, cotes du rhone, dolcetto

COFFEE with SFRAPPOLE

grappa, eau de vie, cognac, armagnac

Three Course Dinner

CROSTONI AGLI ASPARAGI – Asparagus Crostoni

New Zealand sauvignon blanc, pouilly fume or sancerre

MAIALE AL MIELE served with FASCINE DI CAROTE E FAGIOLINI –
Pork Chops with Carrot and Bean Bundles

light medium bodied red, grenache, gamay cru Beaujolais or farmhouse Normandy apple cider

TIRAMISU

Wine suggestions courtesy of Tony Harper. Cru Wine Bar, James Street. Brisbane.

Glossary

Balsamic Vinegar – a sharp-smelling and blackish-brown vinegar made in the Italian province of Modena from the must (fresh juice) of Trebbiano grapes. Traditional balsamic is aged for up to 30 years.

Borlotti Beans – medium large tan bean, splashed with red/black to magenta streaks. Also known as Fava beans

Capers – a small, unopened flower bud picked from a wild bush that grows along the coastlines of southern Italy. Preserved in salt or salted vinegar, capers should be rinsed before using to remove excess salt.

Ciabatta – a crusty Italian sourdough loaf.

Fennel – a feathery topped bulb similar to Dill with an aniseed flavour. The bulb can be eaten raw or cooked.

Gnocchi – pasta dumplings typically made with potato and flour but can be made with cornmeal or pumpkin.

Grana Padano – a less mature and less expensive style of Parmagiano Reggiano

Marjoram – a small leaved herb, often combined with thyme.

Marsala – a fortified dessert wine made using grapes from Sicily.

Mascarpone – a fresh unripened cream cheese that has a slightly acidic, rich, creamy, sweet taste.

Mozzarella – a semi-soft stretch-curd cheese, off white to pale cream colour and usually comes in a pear shaped knob

Pancetta – taken from the same cut as bacon, the belly or cheek of the pig – but air-dried instead of smoked. It can be rolled, aged, salted or smoked.

Parmagiano Reggiano – The king of cheeses produced near Parma and Reggio nell'Emilia in Emilia-Romagna for over 900 years, using fresh unpasteurised cow's milk and aged at least 18 months. Look out for the label stencilled on the cheese as a sign of authenticity.

Penne Rigate – literally meaning feathers these pasta quills have a hollow tubular form cut short on a slant.

Polenta – a very famous dish of the Northern Alpine regions of Italy made from coarse ground cornmeal.

Porcini – spongy wild mushrooms – the Italian name is taken from the word for pigs who forage in forests searching for the mushrooms.

Prosciutto – pork thigh cured through the application of salt, exposure to sunlight, air-drying and aging.

Ricotta – a fresh unripened light-curd cheese made from sheep or goat's milk.

Saffron – the world's most expensive spice comes from the Crocus sativus flower. The fine threads, used sparingly, give dishes a strong yellow colour and honey like flavour.

Sage – one of the most commonly used herbs in Italian cooking. The narrow, tongue-shaped leaves perfume the main component of the dish without overshadowing other flavors.

Savoiardi – long, thick, ladyfinger sponge like cookies with an airy, delicate bite.

Taglietelle – a long flat egg pasta specific to Bologna, cut into 6mm wide strips which expand to 8mm when cooked or 1/12,000 of the height of the 400 year old Torre Degli Asinelli – a tower in Bologna

Tagliolini – a thinner version of tagliatelle made from semolina with a flat, rectangular cut.

Taleggio – a creamy soft cheese with a thin washed rind. Traditionally made in Lombardy, Italy using the same technique since the eleventh century.

Vialone Nano – regarded as the very best variety of short-grain risotto rice it absorbs a great amount of liquid without losing its shape.